FUN-DA-MENTAL
PHILOSOPHY

FUN-DA-MENTAL PHILOSOPHY

*Abolish anxiety and
diminish depression,
with light-hearted
suggestions
and handy hints*

EILEEN LYON

Contents

1. It's Elemental — 2
2. Medical Musings — 7
3. Complementary and Alternative Therapies — 19
4. Animal Encounters — 28
5. Physical Pursuits and Passive Pastimes — 35
6. Relationships — 51
7. Moving Through Life's Seasons — 64
8. Bullying, Self-harm and Suicide — 71
9. Coronavirus (COVID-19) SARS-CoV-2 — 77
10. Facing the Future with Optimism — 84

Acknowledgement — 90

Copyright © 2021 by Eileen Lyon

All rights reserved. Without limiting the rights under copyright reserved above, no part of this publication may be reproduced, stored in or introduced into a retrieval system, or transmitted, in any form or by any means (electronic, mechanical, photocopying, recording or otherwise), without the prior written permission of the copyright owner.

Disclaimer: The author does not provide medical advice or prescribe the use of any technique as a form of treatment for physical, emotional or medical problems without the advice of a physician, either directly or indirectly. The intent of the author is only to offer information to help you in your quest for emotional wellbeing. In the event you use any of the information in this book for yourself, the author and the publisher assume no responsibility.

Any likeness to people, alive or deceased, is purely unintentional.

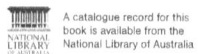
A catalogue record for this book is available from the National Library of Australia

First Printing, 2021

ISBN: 9780645113303 (paperback)
ISBN: 9780645113310 (ebook)

Cover and interior book production:
Pickawoowoo Author Services www.pickawoowoo.com

This is not a medical hand-book. It is a handy book containing a balanced collection of thoughts, ideas and observations. You are welcome to make your own choice about which suggestions to incorporate, and which to ignore, as you proceed to enhance your well-being and contentment.

I

It's Elemental

You and I are quite alike. "What?" I hear you shout, "We don't even know each other." Maybe not, but we're both human beings, and all human beings share about 99.9 percent of deoxyribonucleic acid, better known as DNA. We also have in common a significant percentage of DNA with other animals, the closest being bonobos, chimpanzees, gorillas and orangutans. To a lesser extent, we also share DNA with mice, dogs and chickens! So next time somebody calls me a silly old chook, I won't swear at them. I'll just consider our similarities. (Yeah, right!) Whether you are bright or foolish, grumpy or pleasant, kind or cruel, tall or short, we're all quite similar. In fact, you're as aligned with your worst enemy as with your closest friend. Merely knowing this may make some of you depressed or anxious.

Depression and anxiety are two different conditions, but you may suffer from both at the same time. The realities are that depression and bipolar disorder affect 6.2 percent of Australians between the ages of 16 and 85 each year, and the percentage of Australians of the same age who encounter anxiety in any one year is 14.4 percent. Studies show that mental illness is the third leading cause of disability in Australia.

By depression, I am not referring to the Great Depression which occurred from 1929 –39. I am, of course, discussing the not-so-great depression which lingers perpetually. A depression has been described as a sunken place, the pits, and a rut. The only difference between a rut and a grave is the depth, so it makes sense to exit this gloomy place without delay. Some common symptoms to look for consist of sleeping difficulties, feeling lethargic and lacking energy, unusual moodiness, wondering about death and suicide, feeling guilty or worthless for no apparent reason, not being able to enjoy activities that you previously enjoyed, experiencing eating problems, feeling dispirited and fed up, becoming agitated and being muddle-headed. Each sufferer is different and you probably won't show all these symptoms, but the ones you do recognise will affect your connections with others.

The causes for depression are many and varied, and the combination of several factors may be associated with its development. Incorporated in these are life events such as work stress or job loss, isolation or loneliness, or an abusive, indifferent or threatening relationship (which probably encompasses domestic violence, either physical, mental or both). Some personal factors at play would cover family history, as some people will be at increased genetic risk. However this does not automatically mean the person will experience depression. Your personality could put you at risk if you are self-critical and distrustful, are a perfectionist, a tenacious worrier, are sensitive to personal criticism, or have a low opinion of yourself. Having a serious medical illness can trigger depression in two ways. Firstly, the diagnosis, with its associated tension and fear, and secondly, the long-term management of the illness and the pain and discomfort involved.

Taking certain prescribed medications may also lead to depression. Drug and alcohol use can lead to and result from depression. This is one area that you can control. You know deep down that these substances will not enhance your happiness, so exercise your right to say no. As a rule of thumb, about half of the population with severe mental illnesses are affected by substance abuse.

Anxiety is a troubled, uneasy feeling of distress and apprehension. It can affect all aspects of your health. You may become exceedingly fearful about past and future events, or display an increased dependence on alcohol and/or other drugs. You may develop edginess, nervousness, or irritability and try to avoid unpleasant social situations and your mind may become foggy, making concentration and memory difficult. Anxiety also encompasses a plethora of physical symptoms, which you may or may not experience. This long list includes muscle aches and pains, shortness of breath, shaking and tremors, pounding heart, chest pain, sweating, headaches, vomiting and diarrhoea, or constipation, numbness and tingling, dry mouth, choking, frequent urination, dizziness, blushing, stomach pains and nausea, and restlessness. When the stylist gives you a head massage, you panic, assuming she is compressing your brain, making it less able to perform at its optimum capacity.

It is often a combination of factors that can lead to a person experiencing anxiety. Some of them are the same as for depression and include death or loss, major shock or upheaval, financial difficulties and negative thoughts.

"Heck, this is the twenty-first century," you tell me. "Surely we can blame someone for this bleak news?" Actually, we are all to blame. Yes, that's right, you and I and everyone else, including the posh dude up the road! Society today places huge expectations on us all and shuns anyone who is not 'normal'. But what is normal? Who defines normal? How do we decide where normal behaviour stops and abnormal behaviour begins? Times change, we change, so what was once considered acceptable within a society may not be now, and vice versa. For example in bygone times it was thought to be an extraordinary ability if anyone conversed with the gods, however in our culture we may say they have multiple personality disorder. Special customs which are unique to certain geographical regions would undoubtedly be considered odd to the rest of us. Values and perceptions have changed markedly, and definitions of family and relationships are totally different to what our parents and grandparents accepted as standard. Society has become a lot more materialistic, and mostly we are less spiritual than before. Trying to steer a smooth path through it all is, at times, overwhelming. There's the desire to 'fit in', struggling with the aim to 'be true to yourself'. You've all heard that tired old cliché – think outside the square – but as soon as somebody does publicly, we scream them down. "Blimey mate, you're really weird!" Thus, forcing them to comply, stifling their creativity. Perhaps, being normal involves having the flexibility and strength of adapting as we grow.

I have lived with depression and anxiety disorders (mostly social anxiety) for most of my adult life. Shyness is a heavy-duty form of social anxiety, causing sufferers to feel uncomfortable during social encounters and wanting to escape from them. Next time you see someone looking awkward and not wanting to join in, don't assume they are being aloof. They are probably ill at ease with knots in their stomach. Never before have I felt strongly enough about anything to document it. No, this does not label me a bookmaker! I'm really an accidental author simply wanting to tell my experiences and hopefully help others. My knowledge of writers is very limited, apart from hearing rumours that some of them live a somewhat bohemian lifestyle, taking off to the south of France to rent a villa for several months to get the creative juices flowing and indulging in a few stimulating liaisons. I guess that would be for research purposes. Conversely, my experience did not consist of the above adventures. Before you ask, the reason for my depression/anxiety has nothing to do with missing out on that bohemian initiation! I was recently asked if I have writers' block. I replied, "Of course." That would be the piece of land that my home sits on, right?

2

Medical Musings

After accepting that you have depression/anxiety, the first question to ask yourself is: Do I tell anyone about this? If so, who will I confide in? Maybe family members, friends, work colleagues, or should a health professional be my first port of call? I waited far too long to admit there was a problem, and some of you will do that too. (It's called the ostrich with head in sand syndrome). But heck, that's okay, better late than never! However, the sooner you acknowledge it, the greater your chances of receiving help to enable a full recovery. Mental illness in not a life sentence. Unfortunately, some of us delay seeking help because of the stigma associated with it. As a modern, caring society, we must all strive to reduce this unwarranted stigma.

Be prepared for some non-professional responses when you 'come out' about your affliction. (No, no, not that sort of 'coming out'). Upon hearing your news, a lot of us will feel uncomfortable and unsure of how to react. Some examples of this include, "Are you sure? How do you know?" I really don't know a polite way to answer this one, but does it deserve a polite answer? Next thing you'll probably hear is, "I'm sure you'll soon snap out of it." (Assuming that you snapped into it in the first place). Also, "What you need is a stiff drink." It's never a good idea to self-medicate with alcohol. You will lose friends. As soon as you mention the black dog is nipping at your heels, some folk will run like hell in the opposite direction - perhaps, it means they are afraid of dogs. Initially, when this happened to me, I was devastated, but, upon reflection, I realised I was fortunate to find out because, I didn't need to waste another moment with people who didn't understand. Remaining for you will be the truly genuine friends. Quality, not quantity. When you receive authentic offers of assistance, be sure to accept them. It would be selfish of you not to enable others to encounter the joys of helping. Still, some will carry on as usual, pretending that all is fine. (The ostrich syndrome again.) If you know anyone who you think is experiencing anxiety or depression, please do not ask, "Are you okay?" or anything else that can be answered with a simple yes/no reply. Much better to enquire, "How are you going?" or "Tell me what's happening at the moment." Some folks paint trees blue believing they are supporting persons with mental health issues, but I think they're dreaming. (Maybe barking up the wrong tree?) When you are suffering with the blues, probably the last thing you want to see is a sky-coloured overload! If it was shown to be effective, then surely we would soon be surrounded by whole cobalt forests, or smart scientists would genetically modify the seeds to grow blue trees. Instead of painting dead trees, the live ones could be coated in blue hues, and in time, little sapphire saplings would sprout up all over the place! But humans would still be struck down with mental illness. However, that said, the tree painting doesn't appear to be harmful and could prove beneficial by getting groups out into the fresh air, communicating with others and being active. Maybe next time they will add some different hues to their palette?

Some folks will smother you to the point of almost suffocation. This is where tact is very important. If you don't want visitors for a time, make your feelings crystal clear. I had a few weeks where I just wanted to hibernate at home - lying doggo. Most respected my request, except one woman, and she simply wasn't a friend, barely an acquaintance of an acquaintance. (Brings to mind another saying – There's a rat in every sack.) She did not get a foot inside the door, but I could have directed a foot elsewhere! This was the saddest time of my life and my progress took a nosedive. It was a major setback which left me at my lowest ebb. I felt I must be utterly worthless as my wishes were not being respected. My thoughts became as dark as the deepest corners in a despot's mind. (Another saying – gutted to the gizzard.) Later it was explained to me that she is a very pushy individual who cold calls heaps of others. Pushy people are not pleasant people. It was certainly challenging fighting off the black dog and the intruder simultaneously. Unfortunately, it didn't end there - she began stalking me by email, with the situation becoming so bad I had to change my email address. Sounds easy but then I needed to notify those who I did want to remain in contact with. Awfully time-consuming! This period was the most depressing, experiencing my darkest thoughts ever, which I still can't bring myself to air publicly. At this point, I engaged selective memory loss as a coping mechanism. If you ever find yourself or somebody you know in this situation, don't let it fester. Bring in the heavies straight away! (Call the dogs off). I wonder if these perpetrators ever acknowledge or reflect upon the sadness they inflict on others. Their actions produce a flow-on effect, like a tsunami or tidal wave, and indeed as damaging. Bullying, including cyber bullying, and other forms of violence and nastiness have caused far too much distress and unhappiness to many men and women.

After a lot of time procrastinating, and hoping that this whole damned depression/anxiety thing will magically disappear, you pluck up the courage to visit your GP. This is the point where you are acknowledging you have a problem, and are taking control to improve your mental wellbeing. This will be a bit like a lottery. Some medicos are very helpful and some are hopeless. You may need to visit several before you locate one you're comfortable with. But, hang in there! It is worth the effort. These days a visit to a GP is fraught with all manner of problems. I blame those darned computers! If you have a name similar to another of their patients, they will inevitably pull up their details on the screen. Through this, I've learnt a lot about other patients' health problems, without them knowing. It can be quite funny at a social gathering when you ask, "Is the new treatment for your haemorrhoids working?" They think I must be psychic before they turn psycho! Some patients feel uncomfortable with a diagnosis, so seek a second opinion. This is extremely difficult to obtain because once that blasted computer is turned on there it is – the previous practitioner's appraisal. This causes quite a dilemma. Should they agree with that, or go out on a limb with a different opinion? If so, they will need strong supporting branches.

It is immensely important to book your appointment as early in the day as possible. This helps to ensure that your GP won't be delayed too long, as a prolonged wait will add to your feelings of stress and unease. To allay the nervousness when awaiting to be called in, take a distraction with you. This can be something to read, a puzzle, worry stone, stress ball or anything that distracts you. Taking a Rubik's cube works for me. I will probably never solve it, but it keeps me engrossed and I make delightful coloured patterns. My first GP contact was tremendously disappointing. Unfortunately, my usual GP was unavailable, so I was sent to a younger, newer version. If you're fortunate enough to attend a large practice, demand to see a senior GP. I told him my problem, assuming that I would receive some sort of assistance. But no, he sent me out the door with a questionnaire to be filled in and returned. My next stop was the office where I shredded the silly questionnaire. It now forms part of the wings on a papier-mâché dove which adorns my desk. His offer of a return visit was never taken up! He is still practising. He needs to, diligently! In a perfect world they would work under a no fix, no fee scheme. If you find a helpful GP, he may refer you on to see an advanced health professional, such as a psychologist, psychiatrist, counsellor, mental health nurse, case-manager, mentor or social worker, or an occupational therapist. They will take you through a structured program. To ensure the best outcome, a holistic approach is needed, treating the illness whilst considering the complete person. If you don't feel comfortable with any professional that you are referred to, don't continue with them. There are plenty to select from, and from time to time you will encounter personality conflicts. No problem, swap to another because it is your health at stake here. For instance, an assertive professional could arouse more anxiety, not ideal for your recovery.

A psychologist studied the behavior of humans and animals at a university, realising that it is the human brain that makes them think or act the way they do. They would be provided with supervised technical experience and would be registered with the national registration board. They do not have a doctorate degree and do not prescribe medication. Psychotherapy, or talking therapy, aims to assist a person recognise and alter disturbing thoughts, feelings and behaviours. It is important that all meetings are patient-centered, allowing clients to manage their sessions, because they know themselves best and can be part of the decision making, if they are given the right help.

A clinical psychologist has done additional training on how to treat people with mental health problems. They can provide psychotherapy, including cognitive behaviour therapy, which assesses a patient's thinking process and how it affects their functioning. By changing thinking processes, they are able to change negative behaviours, sometimes finding that imitation and role play contribute to this. A psychiatrist is a practitioner who specialises in treating mental illness. A GP can refer a patient to a psychiatrist if they are very sick or take a long time to recover. They can give you medicine to help with this condition.

Counsellors can provide psychological care, but are not registered with the government, so they may not be fully qualified. Unless a counsellor is registered with Medicare, you cannot apply for a rebate on their fees. Case managers work primarily with clients with excessive or complex mental illnesses. They will work with other members of the medical team to monitor the mental health of their clients, sometimes suggesting alternative therapies and reviewing their medications if necessary.

Mental health nurses are registered nurses who specialise in caring for people with mental illness, especially those with serious illnesses, either in a hospital or in the community. They can provide medical help, practical help and counselling. Social workers are trained and able to provide advice to clients and assist them in practical ways by referring them to other services that they can benefit from.

A trained volunteer mentor can help be assisting clients reach out to support agencies, and will accompany them as they try to increase their independence by participating in community activities. They will be kind and take the time needed to guide their clients forward. Any information disclosed to them will be kept confidential. Mental health occupational therapists provide safe and effective strategies to help their clients understand their ongoing issues, and help them move forward.

Online help is available 24 hours a day, providing you with a directory of free or low-cost health and community services in your area as well as offering fact sheets and downloadable tool kits. Some telephone helplines are also available 24 hours a day, where you can chat to a trained assistant who will listen attentively before imparting some helpful advice to you. They can be suitable for some sufferers but others gain more benefit from direct contact with qualified staff. Alternatively, you could search the internet to find what's available, either in hard copy or electronically, or visit a well-stocked bookstore. If they don't have what you want they will usually order it in. Your local library may also contain some helpful publications.

Local support groups, sometimes called self-help groups, can contribute to improving someone's overall welfare by supplying them with a safe, caring forum to communicate with others in similar circumstances, sharing observations in a non-judgemental way. Confidentiality is paramount, enabling you to share your innermost stories when you are ready. You can start out slowly until you become more accustomed to the group. If you're not comfortable when first attending the group, you can take a trusted friend along with you. Before long, you'll be joining in the discussions, gaining confidence and enjoying the company of your new-found friends. However these groups are not for all, as some participants do feel that they take on the woes of others, making them feel worse.

Psychiatric assistance dogs (also known as service dogs) can provide security and companionship. They are trained to assist their handlers in public, and have access to all public places, including public transport, by way of the Commonwealth Disability Discrimination Act 1992. There is a strict selection process involved, both for the handler and the dog. At the time of writing, these dogs are not readily available across many parts of Australia. Another type of animal therapy is where volunteers take specially trained dogs into health care facilities, including mental health facilities where they provide unconditional love and attention wherever it is needed. Simply by interacting with the dogs some patients expressed feeling calmer.

Virtual reality therapy involves creating an artificial environment, providing a scenario as close as possible to the cause of their concerns, giving the patient a simulated experience which can be used to diagnose and treat psychological conditions. Clinical hypnotherapy is performed by trained, licensed practitioners to treat psychological and physical problems. It is an altered state of awareness, perception or consciousness.

There are mental health retreats in many areas of Australia and overseas where you can enjoy a safe and peaceful stay, often in picturesque surroundings. Usually, they have auxiliary professionals on hand, and offer a range of traditional and complementary therapies, including massage therapy which can be very relaxing if you are a touchy-feely type of person. Massage has been used in Asian countries, especially China, for thousands of years. When we are stressed, our bodies stiffen, our joints tense up and we feel discomfort, which is evident to the observer. Numerous studies show that massage therapy enhances the sense of general body wellbeing, making it an acceptable addition to an existing treatment program. Many different types of massage are available, and some can be done without the need to remove any clothing. Massage strengthens the connection between the mind and the human body, and it is generally quite harmless for participants.

Sometimes, these retreats are technology and alcohol-free zones. "What?" I hear some of you shout. "That's a great idea," is another's point of view. A different type of retreat is a care farm where guests have the opportunity to integrate fully with the animals and gardens, known as 'eco or green care'. They are fairly new to Australia, so as yet there's not many operating. Said to offer structured and supervised programs, they provide educational, social and health services. Some retreats are eligible for rebates through Medicare and private health insurance.

At the time of writing, studies are being conducted to determine whether medicinal marijuana would be useful in treating mental disorders such as anxiety and depression. These trials will continue to involve more patients over a period of time. Another trial at an Australian hospital is the use of psychedelic assisted therapy for terminally ill patients experiencing anxiety or depression, perhaps using psilocybin (found in magic mushrooms) and MDMA. Very low doses (about 5 - 10 percent) of the active ingredient will be used. It is expected that access to this will increase treatment options, giving all patients a greater choice.

Transcranial magnetic stimulation and electroconvulsive therapy are sometimes used to treat severe depression. They alter neurotransmitter levels and receptors and also escalate intensities of restorative proteins. ECT applies direct currents to the patient's head while they are sedated. It is only used if many other treatments have been unsuccessful because of the risk of serious side effects. TMS triggers the brain's healing process in a more moderate way by magnetically stimulating a very distinct part of the brain. It has less side effects than ECT.

The earlier you seek help, the sooner you will be travelling the highway to healing. By seeking help you are not letting this affliction define you but are taking control of the rest of your life. We all have our own ideas of what recovery means to us. Usually, it means you will live a remarkable life and return to good health. You will become more grateful for what you have, and not continually seek additional material possessions. The attitudes and beliefs that society has about mental illness have a powerful impact on someone's illness and their recovery. Of course, this also covers the many articles about mental health that we see in all forms of media, which can be powerful and at times misleading.

Even with this extensive array of help available, we still hear very sad tales of desperate souls who self-present with mental health problems but are turned away and not admitted. Why?

Is it lack of compassion, facilities, trained staff, understanding or finances? Surely, if anyone makes the courageous decision to attend one of these facilities, they should be attended to without delay and referred to a qualified practitioner who can assist them. The staff should pay full attention to what family members of the patient tell them, as they have usually witnessed the distressing behaviour first-hand. Unfortunately, if not assisted promptly and properly, these sufferers may resort to self-harm and/or harming others.

3

Complementary and Alternative Therapies

Simply opening your curtains to let the natural light into your home will make a tremendous difference to your mood. The darker your surroundings may mean the darker your disposition. Maybe you could have some skylights installed. They can be covered easily during the dog days of summer when the heat becomes oppressive. It is also advantageous to open the doors and windows regularly to gain the benefits of fresh air. But if a storm is looming it's okay to close everything.

Something as easy as eliminating many of the chemicals in your home and surroundings can prove to be very beneficial. It is not complicated to make your own cleaning products at home, using basic natural ingredients. An online search will provide all the details and recipes you'll need. If you are time poor, you can usually buy them locally or online. The same applies to cosmetics, as many of the commercial varieties contained a cocktail of harsh chemicals. Thankfully now we have a wider variety of natural alternatives.

Getting enough sleep is absolutely essential to maintaining a good quality of mental health. Most studies tell us that adults require between seven and nine hours per night, but you may need more or less than this. Slumber experts have suggested we go to bed and get up at the same time always, in order to maintain a regular circadian sleep-wake rhythm. Personally, I'm not entirely convinced of this as each day of our lives is different. If we stick to such a rigid routine then surely our lives must be a bit pedestrian. There will often be late night sessions whether they be for study, work, partying, unexpected emergencies, or romantic trysts. Alternatively, there will be times when you're totally exhausted (dog-tired) and you bomb out early, so I'm of the opinion that it's okay to stagger bedtimes. It has been stated that you can improve your chances of nodding off by shutting down all electronic screens at least an hour before bedtime. Yet, the many who doze off in front of the telly will probably disagree. Some people swear by a warm bath, or chocolate drink. You need a comfortable bed and the room temperature must be temperate. Lavender oil is said to produce a calming effect and some folks place a drop of it on their pillow. If possible, make your mind go blank - some of us have no trouble at all with this - relaxing all body parts in turn, starting from your toes, or the top of your head, whichever suits you. It is important not to become alarmed if you have some restless nights, as that won't help. I like to believe that we do catch up eventually. However, if you go a really long time without adequate shut-eye, you may choose to see a sleep specialist. They have rooms where you can stay overnight, attached to wires, and they will monitor your sleeping patterns.

Minimalist living has become very fashionable at the moment. It works on the 'less is more' concept, and is designed to declutter your life. The belief is that by getting rid of unnecessary possessions, you could move into a smaller home, thus saving money. By selling your unwanted items you are immediately increasing your cash flow, which can be used to live a life based on encounters instead of possessions. Only retaining the items that are useful in your life will enhance your budgeting and bookkeeping through fewer transactions. Whilst you're in this clean-out phase, consider any outdated ideas and beliefs you've held onto for too long. Erase them from your thought processes. The same applies to any friends who don't add quality and happiness. Time for a cull. By clearing out what doesn't matter, you're making space for what truly does, increasing your wellness and contentment.

Meditation and mindfulness can have a beneficial and calming effect on some patients. During meditation the mind is absolutely focussed, which is said to improve concentration and learning when practised regularly. Mindfulness is very much being alert in the moment now, acknowledging and accepting your thoughts and feelings. There's been an escalation in the number of meditation and mindfulness apps being downloaded as people can access them readily in their own homes. These spiritual practices are not for all of us, with a small number of participants actually feeling fearful or anxious whilst taking part because, they can be a little difficult to learn. I recently learned of an Australian study claiming 43 percent of Australians aged 65 and over play video games. Digital games are a fun way to unwind and de-stress, and as there are many different electronic games for you to learn, your confidence will get a boost whenever you master a new one. For those with active imaginations, watching science fiction programs can be mind-blowing. Not only are the stories out of this world, but it is fascinating to marvel at the props and costumes, and how did they invent a creature like that? These shows usually provide us with spectacular scenery to concentrate on when we're feeling scared by the action.

Hypnotherapy has been shown to reduce anxiety, stress and fear, and can also be used to treat the symptoms of panic disorder. Self-hypnosis and hypnotherapy allow you to start thinking in the same ways as people who are not suffering from depression. Even so, about a quarter of the population cannot be hypnotised. It is understood that the brains of those who are able to be hypnotised are different from those of those who are unable to be hypnotised.

Herbal remedies are sometimes used to treat depression and anxiety disorders, nevertheless you should always check with your healthcare professional first, as they may not work in harmony with your usual medications. St John's Wort may assist management of stress and mild anxiety. Some other herbal products that could possibly be helpful include Omega 3 fatty acids, saffron, folate and zinc. A varied diet may eliminate the need for supplements.

Sound therapy entails listening to specially recorded calming music through headphones for a short time daily, in a quiet place. By choosing music that works for you, such as classical music or the sounds of nature, you can effectively lower your stress levels. The slower the tempo, the more relaxed your muscles will become. The same results can probably be obtained by playing a favourite CD whilst partaking in low impact activities at the same time. Sound bathing is a practice where a teacher uses a combination of instruments, creating sound waves that emit vibrations, raising the frequency within the body, making you calmer and more relaxed. If you prefer, you can go online and take a weekly class at home.

Qualified art therapists can be extremely helpful by providing a quiet place to express your feelings through free-flowing art. You don't need to be 'the artistic type' because the pleasure is in the activity, not the end result. Art is a form of self-expression which has the ability to calm the nervous system by shifting our attention to focus on what we are creating. The simple act of doodling (no, you naughty person, not that sort of doodle), also known as scribbling or squiggling, is relaxing because of its repetitive sketching.

For many years animal assisted therapy, or equine assisted therapy, has been undertaken in several countries, and although not a lot of studies have been conducted, it appears to help by relieving harmful thoughts, developing trust and being totally alert to your present surroundings, thus decreasing stress levels. Your communication with horses does not need to involve riding them, you may be happy to feed and groom them, or muck out their stables.

Great pleasure can be gained by participating in any hobbies that both challenge and delight us. This can be very soothing, like listening to chamber music, or something really exhilarating like sky-diving, or anything in between. For me, listening to and playing music is always very therapeutic. I love listening to *Roar* at full volume. So hot, the singer should be called Katy Peri-Peri! Singing along to the radio can be particularly enjoyable, as some song lyrics are really upbeat, putting us in a positive headspace. This happy-go-lucky music does make us feel good. Unfortunately, some lyrics can have the opposite effects. Decide on your music wisely as there are some really dark ditties out there. You know the ones where boy meets girl, they fall in love, they fall out of love, boy gets gun, then shoots girl, plus extended family. This is the type of music usually played on Sunday morning country and western shows on radio. Lively instrumental numbers make great listening and it is such fun to make up your own lyrics! Brain games, such as crossword puzzles, including cryptics, Sudoku, jigsaws, wonder words, quizzes, mahjong, Scrabble, suguru, bananagrams and the humble bingo session provide great enjoyment for many. The variety of puzzles is enormous so you can change your selection to provide extra challenges.

Cooking is a stimulating and useful hobby. Yes, we all need to eat! It encompasses the skills of maths, time-management, decision making, dexterity, planning and (every now and then) problem solving. From deciding on your chosen menu, to shopping for ingredients, then preparing them, cooking them, right through to serving and eating, followed by cleaning up afterwards, you are certainly giving your grey matter a good workout.

Reading for pleasure can increase self-confidence, decrease symptoms of depression, help build enhanced relationships with others and reduce anxiety. Reading, whether it be fiction or non-fiction, allows us to understand how others are thinking and feeling. We realise that others are experiencing the same encounters that sometimes challenge us, allowing us to stabilise our feelings and every so often showing us solutions, instead of telling us. If you are an avid reader, you may want to join or start a book club in your area, thus forming a close-knit community based on common interests.

Writing is a very time-consuming pastime. It will keep you so engrossed that you will block out all other thoughts. Whether you write poetry, short stories, romance stories, crime fiction, erotica, history, non-fiction, children's stories, self-help articles, doggerel verse, anything is fine. When you've decided on a story idea, you'll write your first draft which will be revised again and again, and again many times before a final rewrite and decision on the title. Once you get started, you can leave your work, then return to it any time you feel like it. There will probably be countless hours of research involved, and you will be encouraged to look after your health meticulously, as you will have to live a long time to complete your work! If you wish to become published, you will get to undergo the delights of editing, proof-reading, designing the cover, formatting and deadlines to name a few of the obvious, often lengthy steps in the process. This is where I really panicked – I thought they meant dead Lyons! Will you go with the traditional publishing option where the publisher offers you a contract, giving them the rights to publish your book, and paying you royalties from sales, or will you self-publish? The internet has a great deal of information on both options, and talking with published authors will give a personal view of what they've done and why.

The F Word. When discussing our wellbeing, we must take into account the significance of a well-known four-letter word. How much do we need, how often, and what varieties will help us perform at our best? Yes, food is very important, and having a healthy diet is essential for our physical and mental health. By incorporating foods from the five food groups into our everyday eating plan we're certainly giving our bodies a healthy boost. The basic five food groups are: 1. Vegetables and legumes, which contain vitamins, minerals and dietary fibre. 2. Fruit, containing vitamins and dietary fibre. 3. Grains and cereals. Wholegrains have dietary fibre, minerals and vitamins. 4. Lean meat, poultry, fish, eggs, tofu, nuts and seeds, beans and legumes, contain protein, minerals and vitamins. Nuts and seeds also contain dietary fibre. 5. Milk, cheese and yoghurt, and their alternatives. Milk contains proteins, vitamins and calcium. Most of you will recall this information from your school days.

You should still allow yourself treats occasionally, whether you crave chocolate, icecream, cake, etc. When I was growing up, a well-known icecream company had a great slogan for its product, calling it "the health food of a nation." They would never get away with that today, but I so wanted to believe it! The idea is to experiment and have fun with your food choices. If you want a mug of soup and cracker biscuits for breakfast, go ahead and enjoy it. The sun will still come up tomorrow. You may have some definite ideas of your own about dietary matters. If so, that's fine. You can take this paragraph with a grain of salt. If you are following a trendy new-age diet, you can omit the salt, as well as the sugar, and the carbs, and fats, and vegetables that grow below the ground, and anything that was planted on a Sunday.

4

Animal Encounters

Animal companions have proven to be very beneficial for many of us, with an endless choice of possibilities. They teach us a lot about love, loss and death. They can also lower our stress levels and help us fight infections, according to US researchers. I don't like the term 'pets', as petting conjures up another image entirely! Cats and dogs can be very affectionate and loyal. Statistics show that about half of Australians share a home with at least one dog or cat. By going walkies with your dog, you're not only exercising, but also engaging in the community. There is plenty of scope to join a dog walking group or take it to obedience classes. You will also research what is the healthiest diet, the best grooming methods, the many housing options (which may include in the dog-house), and which vaccinations are needed and when. Checking out the local vets to see which one you and your buddy friend are comfortable with is a sensible move, and you'll need to consider whether to take out pet insurance as a safeguard against future illness and accidents. Having your animal desexed and micro-chipped is advisable, and medication against worms, fleas, ticks and lice will certainly make their life and yours more comfortable. Other considerations, depending on what type of animal you pick out, would include health checks, grooming products, bedding and toys, and maybe registrations. Some outside services are available to help when you're temporarily unable to provide for their creature comforts. These cover in-home carers who pet-sit at your place while you're away, dog walkers and foster carers who will look after your favourite fauna at their own home.

Studies in residential health-care facilities have shown that when residents have the opportunity to look after hens and other poultry, their physical and mental health is enhanced, with reductions in depression and loneliness. They participate in all aspects of the birds' comfort including feeding, cleaning out the enclosure and collecting the eggs. Some of the residents will also help in the kitchen, choosing recipes and preparing the eggs for the table. I'm sure that you would gain the same benefits by keeping a few chooks in your suburban backyard. And you would be considered a 'good egg'.

Rabbits and guinea pigs (not the human variety) only require a secure enclosure, a healthy diet and water, but can breed prolifically so either stick to one, or have them desexed, or do both to be really sure. Both will have problems with their teeth if not fed the correct diet. Rabbits require twice yearly vaccinations and their hutches need frequent cleaning. Guinea pigs are quite sociable and noisy, also preferring a hygienically clean enclosure. Ferrets are illegal to keep in

Queensland and the Northern Territory but are welcome in all other parts of Australia. They also need an escape-proof coop, and desexing is extremely important as it goes a long way to eliminating their overpowering odour and prevents the females from succumbing to aplastic anaemia. In summer they must be kept cool as they are susceptible to heatstroke. When treated with kindness they can be quite playful and friendly.

Rats and mice make appealing household inhabitants. They should be kept in roomy wire cages, which must be frequently cleaned and disinfected. Both are intelligent, entertaining and curious, with mice being more timid. Rats can be toilet trained, it has been noted, whereas mice can't. Both are a bit smelly, and the usual advice regarding pet insurance, vaccinations and medications applies.

Aviary birds come in many varieties and colours. Some have a beautiful warble, while others can be taught to speak, although I'm not sure why. There is a large variety to choose from including finches, canaries, quails, budgerigars and many larger types of parrots. Many of the bigger varieties are long-lived providing you with companionship for several years. Depending on the size of your aviary, you can keep any number of avian friends. Yes, size really does matter!

Orphaned lambs will bond with you very quickly, but you must be prepared to feed them every few hours, day and night! If you have the willpower to resist the temptation of roast lamb, they will soon grow into large sheep which can become quite boisterous and knock you over. I've heard that goats (except scapegoats) will also give you much enjoyment but beware, they are inclined to eat whatever they come across. (I kid you not!) Like sheep, they require a lot of room, so are not suitable in high-rise apartments.

If you are pushed for space you could try a hermit crab as they only need a very small home, and don't make a noise. In fact, in a unit where it is stipulated 'no pets allowed', you could probably manage a hermit crab. (Remember to hide it in the wardrobe during inspections).

There's so much scope for animal varieties. It doesn't matter whether your preference is a funky pheasant or a motley mouse. Instead, you may choose to befriend the wildlife that inhabits your local area. This may involve native birds, possums, kangaroos, reptiles, etc. Put a dish of water out for them. Now and then you could feed them, but this should only be occasionally as they must not become reliant on handouts. In some areas you're not permitted to feed native animals.

Aquariums filled with tropical or goldfish are visually appealing, but it must be noted that tanks need regular cleaning and pumps need attention. If you're in an area that's prone to power blackouts, you could lose fish on a regular basis. Don't give them names straight away, as they may not be with you for very long. Goldfish in a fish-tank look a lot more appealing than silverfish in your drawers! If you prefer to keep your fish outdoors, a water trough or old bath will make a suitable receptacle for them. You will need to cover their home with a fine mesh to keep them safe from predators, and provide shelter from the hot sun.

Your animal companions can lead you onto other artistic pursuits, like photography and drawing or painting. You may decide to join a club, enrol in a course or purchase an instructional manual to follow this further. Sculpture and papier mâché can be fun ways to make a replica of a beloved animal.

For a slightly different animal friend idea, you could build a snail house. This is relatively easy to achieve. You will need a small aquarium, or similar container, cover the bottom with soil and sow a few small leafy plants, preferably vegetables and herbs, then collect your snails. If there's not many in your garden, I'm sure the neighbours will happily supply some of theirs! If you want to personalise them, you can paint and decorate their shells. Throw in a few juicy food scraps to keep them happy. You will need to cover the snail home with a strong mesh roof to ensure they don't escape. This will keep the neighbours happy! If your snails are very happy and healthy, they may breed in captivity, so what will you do with the surplus? Some gourmets enjoy eating snails, a culinary delight! But you wouldn't want to consume your little friends, would you?

An ant house is another novelty idea. You could purchase a plastic one from the toy shop or make one using a few common household items. This is a relatively easy task. Searching the internet will provide all the details, then in a short time you will be intently observing these busy little creatures as they live and work together, eating plants, wood and dirt. You will notice that some ants bite, while other sting.

Another option to consider is helping out a rescue group. These wonderful folk rescue sick and injured wildlife, and (all being well) nurse them back to health. Your duties may include collecting the injured animals, preparing their feeds, providing bedding, cleaning their housing or administering medications. There are opportunities to foster or adopt as, unfortunately, not all animals can effectively be re-introduced into the wild.

For a faux pet, you may acquire a pet rock. They are sold in some novelty stores, or if you're feeling adventurous, you could go outside, select a rock, bring it in (adopt it) and paint it to your liking. Pop it on a shelf, in a prominent position, and look at it occasionally. You may talk to it, if you wish. It probably won't answer back! ("Better than some kids," I hear you say.)

When you visit a zoo or wildlife park, you are already helping them simply by buying an admission ticket, as they are raising money for conservation and research. These organisations perform a very important service by housing endangered species in habitats similar to where they would live in the wild, replicating their diets and breeding them for the purpose of releasing many back into their natural habitat to ensure the survival of the species. As you wander amongst the many species of animals and plants you are increasing your knowledge by quietly observing the outdoor world of nature. You will also notice that this time spent in such pleasant surroundings has lowered your stress levels.

5

Physical Pursuits and Passive Pastimes

Exercise has long been recognised as a complementary treatment for depression. It can decrease depression and anxiety by releasing feel-good brain chemicals (neurotransmitters, endorphins and endocannabinoids), and reduce immune system chemicals that can aggravate depression. A spirited exercise session can help ease symptoms for hours, and a routine schedule may reduce them considerably. Exercise increases your overall health and happiness and has some direct stress-busting benefits, as it pumps up your endorphins. If you're suffering from social anxiety, you can go for a solitary walk or run, or work out on one of the various types of exercise machines in the privacy of your home. By now you're probably wondering, is a leap of faith a form of exercise?

Pilates is a physical fitness system developed early in the 20th century by Joseph Pilates. He called it Contrology. Regular involvement in group sessions is beneficial as it provides the opportunity to socialise, releases natural brain chemicals and increases your mindfulness. A hybrid combination of Pilates and yoga has sprung up, known as yogalates. Yoga is suitable for all ages and abilities. It is a very popular form of exercise for depression and anxiety sufferers, with most participants experiencing a significant decrease in stress and anxiety symptoms. It can be practised either indoors or outdoors. Basically, it involves stretching and core strengthening, and places great importance on breathing, helping to slow down and calm the mind. It's hard to be anxious when you're breathing deeply. There are many different forms of yoga. I would struggle to list them all as I'm more familiar with yoghurt than yoga, but will touch on several of the more popular ones. In 1982, chair yoga was developed to enable those with motion and health issues to take part in an adapted version, whilst still gaining the fitness benefits of a workout. The poses (asanas) used are variations of regular yoga poses, which can be performed either sitting on a chair, or using it as a prop.

Iyengar yoga is very well-known and widely practised. It was developed in India and is believed to be the only method that has a standardised global teacher training program. Ashtanga is also widely used. Being vibrant and quick, it is based on a flowing series of asanas, or body postures. Kundalini, originally known as laya yoga, has been practised in the East for thousands of years. Its name literally means, twisted like a serpent, and over time it develops resilience and greater self-awareness. Yin is a type of hatha yoga, originating in China, using techniques to ensure that humans are in time with nature.

Laughter yoga originated in India and involves prolonged voluntary laughter which is considered to lower blood pressure by decreasing stress hormones and triggering the release of endorphins. These happy, social groups are usually run by a trained laughter leader, and 20 minutes of laughter is the optimum amount needed to stimulate a sense of wellbeing. It matters not whether your chortling is heartfelt or contrived as the overall result is an improvement in your betterment as the feel-good endorphins kick in. Beer yoga (or brewery yoga) is thought to have started in Germany a few years ago. Commonly held in breweries or taprooms, it is an informal introduction to yoga which involves downing a few ales during the session. Some fitness experts have criticised this activity as unhealthy. The same experts are not entirely embracing the emergence of wine yoga which is gaining devotees at fringe festivals. Frankly, I feel that we should applaud anyone who can perform some difficult manoeuvres whilst holding a glass of wine. (Okay, they do take frequent sips, so it's empty by the end.)

Couples yoga (or partner yoga) can be practised with a friend or romantic partner as a way to strengthen your relationship, as you move in sync with each other. It is probably not as relaxing as other forms of yoga, and appears to me to be some form of pre-mating ritual! Some devotees enjoy naked yoga, mostly in the privacy of their own homes, or in natural bushland settings. In some western societies that are more comfortable with public nudity, it is performed in group sessions. If you indulge in this activity you will be a yogi bare.

Some folks opt to exercise with their canine companions so both gain the benefits of a workout. As the 'pet parents' yogacise their canine companions wander around socialising with other dogs and the humans. (Perhaps they also chase away the black dog?) This activity is called Doga. Aerial, or anti-gravity yoga, involves being suspended from the ceiling in a comfy hammock doing weightless moves. The hammock provides support for your body, allowing you to float through your movements. It is actually a combination of yoga, calisthenics, gymnastics and aerial arts.

Hot Yoga, a growing trend in Hollywood, is performed in a hot, humid room. The heat acts to raise the heart rate to make the body work harder. The conditions lead to prolific sweating, but it is considered safe for most yogis. Occasionally, it can lead to dehydration and in extreme cases heat exhaustion or heat stroke. Dark yoga (also known as candlelight, or black yoga) is ideal for shy participants as it is held in a very dim place, allowing them to concentrate solely on their own movements. It is popular in London, and is accompanied by heavy industrial music.

Recently, the popularity of pop-up yoga sessions has increased. These sessions are usually held in public or private spaces which were not originally designated for yoga classes. They are either free to attend, or a donation is sought for a charity. Some attendees particularly enjoy these sessions as they meet different participants by travelling to nearby towns to participate. A recent addition to the yoga varieties is Paddleboard or SUP yoga. It is becoming popular around beachside towns and anywhere there is a sizable pool. Participants start off motionless on the board, then move on to trying other postures. If practised regularly it is said to improve core strength.

Another recent newcomer to the local yoga scene is HIIT (high intensity interval training) yoga. This targets your whole body with tougher inversions which increase your heartbeat and cardio moves to turn up your metabolism. Sauna yoga is now being offered, sometimes performed in infra-red saunas, as well as the traditional steam saunas. The saunas are set at a low enough temperature to provide a comfortable, but still sweaty session. Upon entering the sauna, your feel-good endorphins will release, enabling you to switch off and settle into the movements.

Scientists have discovered that stimulating the brain with transcranial direct-current stimulation (tDCS) during meditation and yoga can help us enter a meditative state faster than we are accustomed to. It is called e-meditation. But, if we speed up meditation, aren't we defeating the very purpose of the activity?

All forms of dancing are known to improve rational elasticity if practised repeatedly, as they provide physical and mental exercise. There are a great many varieties to cherry-pick from including ballet and ballroom to Latin and the many ethnic dances. You may dance purely for pleasure, or perhaps you will train hard to enter a dance sport competition.

Gardening is a relaxing, creative activity keeping you in touch with nature. The benefits of being out in the garden take in reducing depression and anxiety, lowering your blood pressure, and being more able to manage your stress. If you don't have the space for a garden, you can join a community garden scheme. Community gardens provide fresh fruit and vegetables contributing to a healthy lifestyle. By participating you are having fun while spending time outside enjoying the social interaction of working with like-minded folks. Alternatively, you can purchase some indoor plants, either real or life-like. To make them more appealing, you can decorate them with faux birds, nests, butterflies and insects.

A running session can help your whole system as it burns calories, lessens food yearnings and lowers your risk of heart disease. It appears to have a contemplative effect on the brain and can work in a similar way to antidepressants, lessening major depressive disorders by promoting the growth of new neurons in the brain. It may also make it easier to fall asleep at night, thus improving memory, lowering stress levels and defending against depression. Conversely, running on empty could be detrimental to your health! If you are the outgoing type and don't mind the smell of sweat and liniment, you may consider joining a gym. You will need to contemplate how keen you are and how likely you'll attend regularly as gym membership can be a bit pricey. Cycling, in its many forms, is also worth considering. It can be a relaxing way to view the countryside, and the initial outlay is not too great. Once you have your bicycle and helmet, invest in a pair of padded cycling pants. It won't take you too long to see the reason for this! In spite of not having cycled since your school days, you'll be back in the saddle just like before. Recycling is very trendy right now.

Rambling through the woods or forest will be enormously beneficial, with nature having a calming effect on the mind, relieving dissenting emotions. Look upon it as a walk in the park! You may yet turn over a new leaf! A short 20 minute tramp or dogtrot amongst the trees can lower your stress hormone levels, making you less anxious. If you chance upon a snake, don't become alarmed, just slowly walk away from it. If you leave it alone, it will leave you alone. Armed with a pair of binoculars, you could turn this exercise into a bird-watching trip. If you are pleased to observe any birds that you chance to sight, you will most likely want to do this habitually, making you a birder. If you become fixated with needing to spot an increasing number of species each time you venture out, you will be a twitcher. I guess that is because you will become twitchy and disappointed when you can't meet your quota. Occasionally, when birds are nesting they will swoop on unsuspecting bushwalkers, scaring and every so often injuring them. The chief culprits for this frightening behaviour are magpies, but the list of swooping birds comprises plovers, magpie-larks, kookaburras, masked lapwings, butcher-birds, noisy miners and red wattle birds. This is no reason to give up on your outdoor adventures as there are ways to deal with these trespassers. If possible, during nesting times (theirs, not yours), meander in a group, always wear a hat and sunglasses, or safety glasses, for protection, and it is advisable to carry an open umbrella or a stick above your head. My solution is to blow up a balloon and attach it to your hat. The pesky birds see it bobbing about and keep well away. If one does chance to attack, the balloon explodes, kapow! Your peace can then be assured for a long time. You're probably wondering, "But what will the neighbours think?" At first, they may be sceptical, but when they see how effective it is, it won't be long before you have a streetful of balloon walkers.

Backward walking is a fun way to add balance exercise to your day, but please find a safe area to avoid bumping into objects or human beings. If you can manage a couple of hours a week in nature, you are more likely to enjoy higher psychological wellness. Obviously, you don't need to be exercising the whole time. Occasionally you could just stand or sit and observe your surrounds. If you invite an overseas visitor along on your bush stroll, you'll need to warn them about the drop bears! They are a predatory cousin to our cuddly koalas, and are likely to jump down out of trees. To avoid disaster, they'll need to wear a wide brimmed hat, or better still a hard hat, and always carry a jar of yeast spread. (Seemingly that lets the bears know that you aren't a threat. It is a well-known fact that no-one carrying the spread has ever been attacked by them!)

By playing a team sport on a regular basis, you will most likely enjoy team support. By making the commitment to attend training sessions and matches you'll become a trusted addition to the group. Some popular team sports to join are netball, basketball, darts, softball, hockey, football, soccer and rugby. If you're regularly playing hardball, it is highly unlikely you're a team player! If you can play ball sports without becoming a tosser, so much the better.

Swimming regularly builds strength, muscle power and cardiovascular health, as well as keeping the heart rate up whilst taking some of the impact pressure off your body. It helps to maintain a healthy weight, robust heart and lungs as well as toning muscles and building strength as any decent swim coach will tell you. If you haven't installed a pool in your backyard, and the neighbours aren't that keen on sharing theirs, your local council pool may be your safest swimming spot, but some swimmers think of this as the vanilla option, and prefer the exhilarating waves out in the ocean with the added excitement of interacting with dolphins, whales and sharks. Some rivers are safe to swim in, but check first, as some can be murky, and some already have crocodiles swimming in them.

Boxing has many direct health benefits as it is a decent stress reliever. It improves your heart health, body strength and composition and hand eye coordination. You have the choice of just doing boxing training for fun, or moving on to competition in the ring. Martial arts therapy is an unusual treatment for social anxiety disorders and depression because it is a mind-body exercise, involving punching and kicking (including kick boxing), which involves much focus and consistent breathing.

Horse riding is another form of exercise which also allows interaction with your animal companion. You may just settle for leisurely trots through the woodlands or enter competitions. These may comprise dressage, cross-country and show jumping. Polo is another option. Originally introduced to train cavalry units, it was referred to as the 'gentleman's sport', or the 'sport of kings'. We are now in the 21st century and it can be played by anyone who can afford the obligatory steed, mallet, ball and protective gear. I guess that now it could also be the 'sport of queens' as well! It is a pretty expensive activity to own a horse, as you will need to feed it, house it and groom it, and there will be vet bills for which you will probably consider taking out pet insurance. Then there are saddles, bridles, horse rugs and horse-shoes. A horse float will be needed to transport it to various locations for competitions, and you may need a larger vehicle to pull it. For yourself, you may need to buy a helmet, some fancy jodhpurs, jacket and boots.

Fishing has been called a relaxing hobby, although obviously not for the fish! It is relatively cheap to get into as you can make do with a hook, line and sinker, as well as some bait and burley. If you can afford the outlay, you will be able to indulge in a fancy boat with trailer and brand-named fishing rods, but you won't be assured of any greater fish catch. You can spend hours serenely waiting and hoping for a jerk on the end of your line (the other end), which will either make you very calm, or very bored. The ebbing and flowing of the waters is a tranquil motion to watch. If you are vegan, you may not wish to indulge in angling because it usually involves killing a living creature, unless you are the 'kiss and release' type. (You may not be a fisher, but still you are that type?) I wonder just how many of the released fish actually survive. After releasing it, you can still brag about your catch. It was how BIG?

Travel can be an enjoyable activity, although in the current viral environment people are a little wary of venturing too far from home. When it is safe to do so, tripping around offers many choices of scenic destinations, and your trip can be as peaceful or as adventurous as you wish. There is a vast selection of holiday options to consider. If you are super self-confident, then being a solo traveller would offer you the most flexibility to come and go as you please. Maybe you wish to travel as a couple. This works best if you have similar interests. You may have a group of friends to travel with, but this will involve a fair bit of give and take. ("Yes, we'll visit those three museums today, but tomorrow it's bungee jumping.")

Another alternative is booking with a registered travel agent on an escorted tour. (No, no, not that type of escort!) This means all the details have been taken care of, leaving you free to just participate and enjoy. It's best to start off by going on a short accompanied trip to see if it suits you. It may be that some of your fellow travellers are as noxious as a boozer's burp, making a week touring with them seem more like a month. Also, the tour may be extremely regimental, with strict adherence to meal times, travel times and time spent at each stop.

The next consideration is how you wish to travel. Flying in an aeroplane is definitely the quickest, but the very thought of drifting rapidly through the clouds is enough to leave some travellers feeling ill. Cruising aboard a large ocean liner is certainly more leisurely, but not advisable if you're prone to sea-sickness. Also, some passengers can become claustrophobic since there's no ready escape available. Tourist coaches are now enormously comfortable with most of them fitted with seatbelts and toilets. The bus driver will regularly give a commentary about the area that you're travelling through. Train travel is popular, with some being fitted out with sleeping cabins and restaurants. You could, of course, drive to faraway destinations in your own car. Usually, this doesn't prove to be very relaxing if you're too busy watching traffic to appreciate the scenery. Also, it does require a knowledge of reading maps properly! A vacation that covers a few different modes of travel would be most exciting.

To gain the most from your sojourn away, you will need to engage proper holiday mode by cancelling out all thoughts of what is happening back home. It is essential to cancel all newspapers. Don't have them saved so you can waste your time back home by perusing stale news. Chances are if you weren't there, it doesn't concern you. If you need to know, someone will approach you upon return. Not taking any electronic devices with you will give you the best chance to forget about home and immerse yourself into the full vacation vibrations.

Watching sport can also be a rewarding pastime. Hence the great Aussie chant - scream for your team! It has a real tribal sound to it, as if you all belong to a wonderful clan. If you can travel along to see the action live at the venue, your pleasure increases tenfold. Wear the team colours and cheer when they score, sigh when they don't. A word of caution – have a plan before you go. Recite this mantra quietly to yourself: "My favourite team has a 50 percent chance of winning today. If they come second, I will not become upset because I will still enjoy the atmosphere and camaraderie of attendance. This is where I choose to be." Always be aware that referees and opposing teams are vitally necessary in order to have a contest. They are human beings, like you, with feelings and uncertainties. If you decide to boo or swear at them, you're revealing a lot about yourself. If distance, illness or finances prevent you from travelling to the game, you can always sink into your favourite comfy chair and watch it on the telly. Nowhere near as great an atmosphere, but you can holler and shout to your heart's content!

Volunteering can be a rewarding experience, and there are plenty of options for you as vollies are generally in short supply. The organisations which use vollies are widespread and take in sporting clubs, schools, hospitals, aged-care facilities, community gardens, special interest groups, service clubs, public libraries, plus many charity groups, and they are also required for special one-off occasions. Check in your local area to see what is available that interests you. Volunteering was a whole lot simpler in a less regulated world. You just turned up, rolled up your sleeves and got on with it. These days you will probably need to apply for a police clearance and a working with children clearance. In some cases, the charity will assist you with this and pay for it. You may be asked to sign a disclaimer stating you won't discuss anything that occurs whilst you're there. By all means, sign it, but if all is not right, then you are morally obliged to report it. Occasionally, you will notice a definite pecking order between the paid staff and vollies. This can cause tension, but can usually be resolved by frank discussion. Prior to approaching your chosen organisation, have a clear vision of how much time and effort you are willing to give, setting the boundaries early. This ensures that you remain a jolly vollie who doesn't turn into a grumpy slave. Before becoming a vollie make sure you are doing it for the right reasons and not for personal glory and fringe benefits.

Another feel-good activity for some folks is donating to a chosen charity. You must do your homework meticulously first. It's not advisable to donate to the strongly accented voice who has just phoned you from Nigeria asking you to help the Worthy Waifs welfare fund. If you can afford to help a good cause, your local area would be the ideal place to start. Find out what is needed in your district. Do you trust and believe in this cause? You must feel completely comfortable because it is your hard-earned dollars you are giving away. Will it be a once only contribution, or do you intend to donate on an on-going basis? Make your intentions very clear at the beginning because some charities will hound you mercilessly once they have your details. Be wary of charities that 'suggest' a suitable donation amount. You are free to donate any amount you select. Don't be bullied into going along with their suggestion. If they stipulate an amount, it's not an offering, it's a fee. Ask questions regarding what percentage of your money will be retained for administration costs.

Still going with the feel-good vibe, you could practise random acts of kindness. These could include anything that you feel would increase the betterment of the receiver. A few popular suggestions include reading to the elderly, as they may want to keep up with the news, but failing eyesight prevents them from reading for any length of time because of eye strain. If you're game, you could compliment a complete stranger on their hairdo, attire, etc. By putting together a food hamper and delivering it to a local charity for distribution, you are providing both food and dignity to those who find themselves needing it. Maybe a resident in your street is doing it tough? Offer to mow their lawn, or do their shopping, or bake a meal for them. The gift of music is likely to be very well received. If you are computer savvy, make a collection of their favourite tunes, downloaded to a USB drive. As these can contain thousands of tunes, they will have never-ending melodies. (Maybe they will sing your praises?) If you want more inspiration to perform these acts of thoughtfulness, there are plenty of internet sites to guide you. A word of caution here – if you continue to do these things too regularly, to the same people, you'll be seen to be brown-nosing. Less is more.

We should strive to obtain a balanced life. There are times when we keep very busy, but we must also schedule in times to chill out. We've dealt a lot with physical activities, so now we'll consider passive pastimes like watching television, reading, playing computer games, sketching, enjoying comic books, looking up current jokes online, quietly listening to music, or whatever helps you switch off. These should be enjoyed frequently without guilt to counterbalance the busyness of life. You've no doubt heard the old saying – All work and no play is not okay, it only causes dismay. There are some popular soap operas on Australian television that have lasted more than 30 years. These are loosely based on real-life scenarios, so can be interesting and informative as well as entertaining. These shows give us a glimpse into the lives of others. By watching the struggles of the characters, we're more likely to realise that our problems are pale by comparison. It is a scientific fact that the excitement we go through whilst watching telly can lead to the manufacture of endorphins in the body.

6

Relationships

Christmas and New Year are the busiest times for mental health problems, including attempted suicides. "Why", you ask, "shouldn't we all be excited and full of good cheer?" Maybe not. As a largely secular society, we've lost our way trying to navigate the meaning of this short break from work, and maybe fitting in a getaway. If you pay attention to the cynics, you probably believe the whole idea is a ploy created by shopkeepers to boost their profits. Unreal expectations are placed upon us at this time, when large related groups, with nothing in common, except maybe a surname, are expected to play happy families for prolonged periods. Sometimes, they feel sorry for folks who are spending Christmas alone, and try to drag them along. How many of us have secretly envied them? Well-adjusted people can actually enjoy their own company. Solitude is a feeling we should learn to feel comfortable with, without guilt. It allows us to pause and recharge, which is vital in today's fast-paced world. There is a great deal of difference between being alone and being lonely.

Another well-known saying – It's better to walk alone, than with a group headed in the wrong direction. Many types of human beings share this planet, and while some may need to be constantly surrounded by troops of people, others would find the whole concept daunting. Some groups are now attempting to boycott Christmas festivities altogether, by not putting up the tree with decorations, or listening to the well-known (well-worn) carols. They journey to distant lands in December where Christmas is not celebrated, and it is just another working day. During this busy period, there are many repetitive festive seasonal parties. A modern young lad recently gave his take on these occasions: You hang about, eating and drinking too much, engaging in small talk, until you find somebody to bonk or fight. By now, you've worked out why it's called Boxing Day!

Then there is the exchanging of gifts. One year, I received 13 calendars! Some were particularly scenic, containing landscapes and seascapes from Fiji, Queensland, Germany, New Zealand and Scotland. Another featured the cutest puppies and kittens that you're ever likely to encounter. One was comprised of semi-nude photos of a local charity group, put out as a fund-raiser. Had they been fully clad, I'm sure they would have sold lots more! There was also the usual assortment displaying tractors, cars and sheds. One displayed monthly affirmations and quotations. These all left me with a dilemma. Which ones to display? I could not decide, so hung up the lot. I did not see the writing on the wall for a whole year!

For some individuals the prospect of a clan get-together has them as excited as a fox in the hen-house. Alternatively, others would become as nervous as a turkey in the lead up to Thanksgiving. You may all start out as friends, but soon you're whipped into a frenzy. Families vary significantly, from bolstering your security and providing comfort and assistance, to constant power struggles and manipulation. (dog eat dog). Most family groups would sit somewhere between these two extremes. It's been stated that blood is thicker than water, also that it is possible to drown in both. In this enlightened age, we don't expect anyone to remain in a romantic relationship that is unhappy and well past its use-by date, so why should we expect anyone to remain in a dysfunctional domestic relationship? Every so often we hear in the media that 'family is everything', which is fine for those who genuinely enjoy the company of their rellies. Yet, it is a generalisation which is overrated. If you belong to a family in which the lines of communication are down, it is still possible to live a wonderful life. Don't dwell on what you don't have, concentrate on what you do have. These days anything goes, so you can make anyone part of your 'family' so long as they agree to it! None of us has the right to be critical or judgemental because we surely don't know all - or sometimes even any - of the facts. Being an individual adult you have the ability to analyse each invitation you receive and not just follow the mob mentality. Most likely you'll find that these outings are not compulsory. A good question to ask yourself is, "Will I enjoy or endure this gathering?" Never feel pressured into accepting anything just to keep the peace. Better to look after your inner-peace, otherwise you may go to pieces! When you are at peace with yourself, you will display a natural compassion to all – people, animals, environment and inanimate objects.

I am tremendously fortunate to come from a small family - one mum, one dad and one sister, all wonderful folks. Also, our extended brood is small. When we shared a joint, it meant sitting around the kitchen table, tucking into roast lamb, baked potatoes, pumpkin and carrots, with green peas on the side and accompanied by gravy and mint sauce. If you're young and modern, right now you're probably thinking, "How quaint. They actually all sat down and ate together!" This wasn't just to make meal service more efficient. It was a coming together to discuss feelings, doubts, triumphs and snippets of each other's lives. Nowadays, sharing a joint involves a foul-smelling substance, which could possibly land you an appearance in court!

Alternatively, some families are really huge and somewhat intimidating. I'll share some of the diverse characters you are likely to encounter. As you read through them, you'll be alarmed at how many you recognise. No, we're not related. There's a definite pattern of human behaviour. There's Uncle Boris, who is quick to criticise us, and teases constantly, because he doesn't fit in. The best way to deal with him is to look him straight in the eyes (you may need to stand on a chair) and ask, "Do you tease because you feel inadequate?" If there's an audience the impact is far greater. He probably won't attend the next gathering but if he does, he'll be as quiet as a dead mouse! Some teasing is light-hearted fun, but most is a subtle form of bullying. Next there's Aunty Sharon, a lifelong spinster, with no children but ever ready to dish out advice on other people's offspring. She'll buy gifts for all ensuring that she's forever included in future gatherings. Distinctly domineering. Next, we encounter the 'good wife/good daughter', easily identified by her desire to be accepted. She'll roll up with tasty home-made slice and help with the washing up, all the while filling the room with her sad-speak, continually moaning about her latest medical problem. Also present is probably the 'superwoman'. This one does it all by herself. Yes, that's correct - baking, sewing, art and craft, gardening, home maintenance, you get the picture. She makes sure that you notice what she does. But beware, it usually means that she has a sordid past she's trying to atone for. Usually in the mix will be an elderly relation still living alone at home long after it is safe to do so. This poor soul is not there for their independence, but because other family members find it convenient. Imagine having problems at home and nowhere to escape to. So off you go to visit the most senior of the species. This person doesn't complain (much) because they've been brainwashed into believing how wonderful they are by coping alone. (with copious assistance from many community services).

You might also have met the copycat offspring – a lap dog - following in their parents' footsteps, most likely choosing the same occupation as a parent. (Despite Dad and Grandpop playing football at national level, we'd admire you more if you followed your true passion - ballet!) This one is forever under the thumb, still obeying their parents long after they've died. Here is a tantalising question for you to consider: Are in-laws any less dangerous than outlaws? Flesh and blood groups may also contain a few who imbibe a bit too much over and over again, and who experiment with dangerous substances. You most likely have come across the perpetual salesperson who is always networking. Most of us have met the 'know-it-all' who has an opinion on all subjects that are discussed. Probably one of the most annoying is the non-stop chatterbox who usually provides us with far too much information. Also present will be the 'free-loader', who will partake of all you have to offer, but never bring a contribution. This one is so mean they probably have two birthdays a year! When they come to visit, instead of earnestly watching the clock awaiting their departure, you desperately gaze at the calendar! There is usually at least one misery-guts. Don't ask this one "How are you?" unless you want a full rundown on each bad thing that's ever happened to them, real or imagined. Sometimes we hear of a person who has died, 'surrounded by his loving family'. Was that a good thing, or did he die because there were so many of them in the room that he expired through lack of oxygen? We need to be wary of descendants who come back into someone's life at the end of it. There is the prodigal son who has led a somewhat curious lifestyle but manages to re-join the group for redemption and a share of the will. Once in a while at the end of a very long line of offspring is the spoiled youngest. Maybe the other family members are so grateful the breeding has stopped that they shower this one with great affection. Or could it be because of how this one turned out that the breeding stopped? Naturally, your perception of the tribal dynamics will depend upon whether you were born into the family, or whether you joined later, either willingly or otherwise!

Let's examine the importance of the common funeral. It's been stated that humankind became civilised when we started to bury our dead. Well, we've certainly come a long way since then! Several of today's funerals have all the pomp and ceremony of a circus carnival and are often attended by countless rubber-neckers who haven't ever met the dear departed. It seems the more gruesome the circumstances of your demise, the more on-lookers will turn up. How many of the attendees are true mourners? Like any public assemblage, the reasons men and women attend are many and varied. What many don't understand is that you don't need to have a full-on public funeral at all. As we are now mostly a secular society, a member of the clergy is not essential, nor is a civil celebrant. Anyone connected to the deceased can preside over the service. It can be as short or long as you wish and can be an intimate private gathering, or no gathering at all. The end result is still the same. The guest of honour is just as dead. Those close to the dear departed could be grieving for many different reasons. Obviously, they are missing the physical presence of the person, but could also be experiencing lifestyle changes and changes in ancestral hierarchy. I find it perplexing that sometimes during the eulogy it is stated that the guest of honour took part in risky behaviour, probably causing his parents much anguish at the time, but as he's now dead, it's looked upon as heroic! Ever notice how even the thugs, womanisers and crooks are portrayed as saints? What message are we giving our young folk? Another worrying trend is the growing number of advertisements by funeral companies. None of us are going to get out of here alive, so they already have a steady stream of clientele. I find a number of the ads displayed on television during prime viewing time to be extremely distasteful. They are more like ads for a full theatrical performance.

Public shrines are another disturbing trend. A temporary monument will be set up at the precise location where the death occurred, usually consisting of flowers, toys and messages. If the tragedy was a traffic accident, the display is often set up close to the edge of the road, causing a distraction for drivers. As with funerals, if the demise was sudden and really nasty, lots of spectators will attend. Yet if this display became the size of a mountain, the casualty will still be deceased. Some of these casualties will have endured a particularly horrific ending. As we will never really understand the mind of the perpetrator of this deed, should we be seen to be exalting their actions? In what way is this collection of objects going to help anyone, except maybe the local florists? Soon, the flowers will wither and die, the toys will deteriorate and the messages will blow away. Next workers will have to come along to clean up the mess. Rather than wasting your money, send flowers to the local hospital or aged-care facility where the living can enjoy them, or offer to help pay for the funeral, because when these unfortunate happenings occur, they aren't budgeted for and can cause hardship.

Following closely behind family relationships would be romantic connections. Your expectations and understanding in this domain will largely be based on what you've noticed in your nearest and dearest, and any personal encounters up to this point. So your upbringing will shape how your feelings about life's encounters will impact you. If you've been brought up to rely on the myth about living happily ever after, you're in for a massive shock. That mostly only happens in the fairy tales. However, it is still possible to continue in a loving partnership for a very long time, if you're both prepared to put in a considerable effort. The romantic notion needs to be tempered with a generous helping of realism! It's been stated that if you desire a high degree of fidelity, you'll need to invest in a top-quality sound system. Communication is the most important ingredient in any relationship. When a couple can communicate openly and honestly with each other, and are mostly in sync with each other, they present a united front to the world, giving them a greater sense of security and confidence. There's an endless list of reasons why partnerships start, including feeling sorry for someone, though this is never a good reason as eventually you'll end up feeling sorry for yourself. Other reasons would be needing to experiment, rebounding, or getting back at parents or peers. A healthy loving relationship is one in which both partners are completely at ease to be themselves, without fear of ridicule, betrayal or violence. "But surely all relationships start out like this?" you ask. They probably do, but things change, and it is how you deal with the changes that determines your mental health wellbeing. Betrayal does not simply mean bonking anyone other than your chosen partner. It also includes sharing too much private information with outsiders, belittling your partner publicly and deliberately ignoring your partner to impress strangers. Love means nothing without loyalty.

To save time when summing up a possible suiter, one foolproof method is to meet at a café or restaurant for a meal. You will learn so much in a couple of hours, enabling you to decide if a second date is wise. Were they punctual? Did they treat the wait staff with courtesy? How did they fill in the time waiting for their meal? Hopefully they didn't play with their phone or become impatient. Could you hold a two-way conversation without interruptions, or did they continually scour the room? When the meal arrived, did they eat quietly and slowly, or did they gobble it up like they'd just come off an extended famine? Payment time comes around and it is perfectly okay to go Dutch on a first date, but if a wallet is missing then the alarm bells should be ringing louder than an air-raid siren. Interestingly, in the sixties and seventies, if a girl wasn't married before her twenty-first birthday, she was considered an old maid. During this era, a lot of young girls literally moved from homework to housework. Thankfully, society and attitudes have changed and couples are marrying much later in life, having undertaken a wider range of careers, partners, travel and other options. A topic for discussion would be: Is marriage, as we know it, still relevant in the 21st century?

Certain families are overly affectionate in public with kissing and hugging on display for all to view, which may be a sign of genuine affection. This does not mean they are any more caring than the quiet, reserved ones. On the contrary, they may feel the need to act out, to cover up deep problems and insecurities in the relationship. These public displays of affection can make others feel uncomfortable, and every now and then the participants are simply showing off. In some countries, overt displays of affection are viewed most seriously.

I am of the opinion that romantic liaisons should be kept private. There appears to be a growing trend towards public proposals. Why? Not really an intimate moment, is it? Public displays of affection are most likely the domain of hedonistic individuals, or couples who should be pitied as they are clearly not at ease with their situation. We certainly hope they don't go to the next step of consummating the union publicly as well!

We are repeatedly bombarded with media reports about physical violence, which can be most noticeable when the victim has terrible injuries, making us feel disgusted and wanting the perpetrators to be punished severely. But what about the subjects of emotional abuse? This is a form of torture. Their scars are hidden inside, sometimes for decades, often without others noticing that something is amiss. Perhaps we should all pay more attention to those around us, and maybe we'll recognise the clues. We should speak up if all is not right.

If breaking up makes you feel as though you have failed, you're more likely to become depressed. One thing you must guard against is playing the victim. Your future is in your hands, so plan it carefully. You could see it as a learning curve, taking away from it any constructive memories, to help you in your next encounter. Yes, there's a likely chance that you will recover and go on to love again. There's a large world out there, so it makes sense to believe that there are many potential suiters. Think of them as friends you haven't met yet. (Or you may give up on this whole darn love thing and become a hermit, whatever makes you happy!) This also applies to changing relationships within neighbours, work colleagues and society in general. If you have a platonic relationship, does it mean you come from different planets?

Any attachment requires bucket loads of compassion, compromise and understanding. The following scenario will provide you with some fodder for thinking. You visit a friend and she ushers you in, eager to show off her latest clothing purchase. She has recently bought a pair of exercise leggings that cling to her body tighter than a distraught toddler. "Does my bum look big in these?" she asks. "Sure does, and your thighs look humungous," you are tempted to reply. But instead you say, "Culottes are in now, let's go and buy some together." You have shown your maturity by choosing kindness over honesty. Right now, you'll be as revered as an elephant in Thailand.

Relationships are formed when we interact with other human beings. All people who deal with the public should have to undergo a compulsory course about compassion, understanding and humility, from shop assistants to bank managers and everyone in between. Can you image how our all-round happiness would soar if this happened? We'd all feel as rapt as a gift in December! Here's a little exercise for you to do. Put this book down now and think about the sheilas and blokes you are close to. Where is the friendship going? Are there equal amounts of give and take? Are you always happy to hear from them? Have you ever been taken for granted, leaving you feeling used and abused? Do you receive back-up and encouragement when it is desperately needed? When you stuff up do they gently remind you that this is a once-only glitch, not a permanent state of being? Most importantly, is this friendship more fulfilling than it was this time last year? Here I must point out that life is sometimes full of promise and sometimes full of compromise. Occasionally liaisons linger past their use-by date because we become lazy and continue out of habit and sentiment. (The boiling frog syndrome.) Be wary of superficial friendships. Just because you've joined fifteen community groups, that doesn't make you popular. Most likely it means you're a try-hard with a few acquaintances, but where will they be when you need assistance? An Australian study has shown that having negative social interactions raises inflammation in the body. Those who initially joined us as a breath of fresh air can easily become an ill wind that blows no good. Memory Lane and Fool's Paradise are great places to visit, but they make an unpleasant permanent location. Sometimes the grass does appear greener on the other side, but then we realise it's been fertilised with BS, which probably means it will peak early then die.

7

Moving Through Life's Seasons

An important mantra to regularly recite is, "I want to live before I die." By living, I don't mean merely existing, but ensuring your days are jam-packed with countless wide-ranging adventures, filling your memory-bank with exquisite images. First step is to accept yourself as you are. We hear so much about the power of positive thinking. It is not a magical solution, and you must be realistic. Even if you are shooting for the stars, there's still a possibility that you'll end up in the gutter! This is when you pick yourself up, dust yourself off and either try again, or decide upon a different course of action. It may be time to engage Plan B. Remember there is usually a chance to try again tomorrow. Whatever you choose to do, give yourself whole-heartedly, keep evolving and always pay attention. At the start of each year a number of us make New Year's resolutions. Most of these will remain unfulfilled. The reason for this is blatantly obvious - whenever you see the need for a life change, make a new life affirmation immediately because if you wait for the next year to begin, you've wasted time and are following the mob mentality.

First impressions are lasting impressions, so think carefully about how you want to be portrayed. You are unique and deserve respect from all others. As this is a two-way street, you are also required to respect those you come into contact with. Don't compare yourself with others, because, thankfully we are all different. Wouldn't life be boring if we were all the same? Do you wish to blend in, or would you prefer to stand out? Decide which then dress accordingly. However, if you decide to make a spectacle of yourself, don't cry foul when someone takes a pot shot at you. There are colour coaches out there who can advise you on which colour clothes to wear to suit your personality. For example, bright colours like red and orange can produce feel-good vibes, while blue is said to have a calming effect. Wearing darker colours may mean having a darker frame of mind. If you really want to wear a certain colour that doesn't suit you, go ahead and wear it anyway. As long as you also wear a huge smile you'll get away with it. Your body language says a lot about you. Do you walk tall with your head erect? Yes. It is possible if you're short in stature. Are your arms relaxed? Don't hide your hands in your pockets or cross your arms in front of you, as this gives the impression you're shutting others out. Remember to use eye contact when conversing with others. Learn to be an attentive listener. Those of us who have social anxiety will often become nervous, so here's a tip that has been known to work. To boost your confidence, tell yourself the person with whom you're speaking likes you a lot. I'm not sure why this works, maybe it's because you portray a certain boldness and self-assuredness. Regarding your social anxiety, it's a good idea to take note of when it mainly occurs. Are you travelling solo at the time, or are you accompanied? Maybe it is your consort who is adding to your stress by not fully supporting you. You may need to part company for a while to see how you fare alone in public. If your confidence comes flooding back, you know what to do next!

You can brighten your outlook enormously by confident considerations. Every day find one thing that makes you happy, and maybe document it in a journal for future reading when you need cheering up. It can be as simple as a chirpy little bird on your windowsill. On the other hand, if all you see is a vicious butcher bird feasting on the baby wrens outside your window, please look away and concentrate on something else – anything else! The radio might be playing a catchy tune which makes you smile, or somebody may email a note totally irrelevant and funny to you. By now you get the picture that it's not too difficult to find a little loveliness each day. After a while, increase this to finding as many great things as you can daily. You'll be amazed at how catching this is. The selfless act of celebrating the success of others fills us with satisfaction and positivity, leading to greater optimism and gladness, and inspires us to strive for our own successes. By engaging a self-assured mindset, we greatly enrich the most boring experiences. Instead of thinking (and saying), "I have to do this chore", think, "I choose to do this now". By putting yourself in charge and rethinking the situation, you've immediately increased the pleasure of the activity.

A successful strategy for dealing with frustrations is to look outward, not inward. Despite what you may imagine most of society isn't really that interested in you. By not taking things personally you won't let them affect you. Be aware that it is perfectly okay to feel bad at times, and this is when to feel compassion for yourself. Sure, you're not good at many things, but I'll bet that you know things that I haven't begun to learn about. Focus on these. When you do well and someone pays you a compliment, accept it graciously with a simple, thank you. Failure teaches us a great deal more than success ever does, usually about ourselves. If you can sometimes learn from the mistakes of others, you will save yourself both time and heartache.

Generally, when we are around others, we are expected to conduct ourselves in certain ways, to fit in to society. As parents, we are expected to provide love, food and shelter to our offspring. As students, we are expected to arrive on time for lessons and study hard. If we work with others, we are expected to do our portion of the task diligently. As friends, we are expected to be attentive and co-operative. By agreeing to follow these ideals, we will have the approval of our peers. We will indeed notice their disapproval, if we don't comply.

These days we all strive to be cool, calm and connected, but too much screen scrutiny can be a time-wasting menace. As a writer (not a rioter), I accept that a computer is a necessity, but I only use it as a tool, not a distraction. Social media and reality TV are designed to make you unhappy. It's been shown that episodes of reality TV have been heavily edited, giving viewers a greatly distorted image. Posts on social media are frequently self-gratifying rubbish. Don't they all look glamourous in those photo-shopped pics? Don't be fooled by any of it. Some people see the writing on the wall while others view only the graffiti. I firmly believe that modern day 'influencers' are just bullies in disguise. If this upsets you, don't use social media. That's right, don't waste another minute viewing such rubbish. I don't, and I'm okay - or somewhere pretty close to it.

Life is meant to be a challenge. Get used to it. If we didn't come up against the crap times, we'd never appreciate the truly remarkable times. By coping with and rising above the difficulties, we build resilience, strengthening our character for the next challenge. The only ones who think that life is a bowl of cherries are the wannabes and drongos, and they just give the rest of us the pips! A handy benchmark for deciding what is important to agonise over is to ask yourself this question: "Will it really matter this time next year?" If not, don't waste time with it. If so, work like a dog at resolving or sorting it out. Give it all you have, then find a bit more.

You may have been born with a silver spoon in your mouth. As you grow older you'll be expected to continually polish the damn thing, wasting a lot of time and energy. Bin it and move forward your own way. Or, you may have been born with only a plastic spoon in your mouth. As your teeth developed, you bit into it, probably using your canines, and choked on it. But you spat the bits out and moved forward.

In general, today's society does not cope well with disappointments and setbacks. As adults, we're putting out the wrong message to children. And they expect to be happy all of the time. This is not a perfect world. It is a real world. Let them learn from an early age that every now and then they will hurt, they will fail and they will become unhappy, but they will learn so much from these experiences, enabling them to become strong and resilient. Empower them to become grown-up, not groan-up.

I hold an unwavering conviction that life consists of four seasons, similar to our weather patterns, with each term lasting roughly about twenty years, or a generation. We are born into life's spring season, the time of birth, growth and renewal, an energetic time when we grow and learn and experiment, and start to blossom, hopefully with a spring in our step. During this season, our bodies change rapidly, all the way from babyhood to puberty and beyond. It's also the prime time to put plans in place for our ongoing health and welfare. This is a happy-go-lucky period involving schooling and maybe further education, junior sport and possibly dance or music lessons, before responsibilities and restrictions arrive.

Soon, our summer has arrived. This is our hottest period, a time of exposure, when we bathe in the sunshine of life, letting our true selves be vulnerable as we become real go-getters, plunging enthusiastically into action, with great lashings of vitality. Our bodies are still developing rather fast and predominantly we're becoming stronger. Commonly, during this time, we may train diligently for and secure employment, enter into a meaningful relationship, become parents, join the armed forces, or decide to volunteer with an organisation which can make a vital change to others or we may not.

Following summer is the autumn of our life, the season of transition, known as middle-age, an unpredictable and changeable juncture, when we can stay fixed in our thinking, or change with the times. Just like the withered leaves falling from the trees, this period of maturity can signal a steady decline. By now are bodies are slowing down as we approach menopause, or manopause. It is a time for counting our blessings and revelling in our achievements. This is our last hoorah before winter.

Finally, we reach the winter of our life, known as the golden years, which is said to be the wettest season, a phase of dormancy and contemplation. This is meant to be a stage of acceptance and with any luck, feeling comfortable within ourselves, when we concentrate on what is really important to us. We may decide to retire from our working lives and take off to see new places and tribes, or we could elect to stay in familiar surroundings amongst family and long-term friends. However, we should not rely on them too much but strive for a fair amount of independence. Our bodily changes are now more noticeable, with some parts needing repairs or replacement.

8

Bullying, Self-harm and Suicide

Self-harm occurs when Homo sapiens deliberately injure themselves, usually without others knowing, and is mostly carried out in private. Generally they are unable to deal with their feelings of misery and gloomy emotions. Many things can trigger self-harm including bullying, anxiety, depression, relationship difficulties, family, school or work disagreements, low self-esteem, alcohol or drug dependence and sexual woes. Some may do it only once, whilst others will make a habit of it. This is done as a way of replacing emotional pain with physical pain. Mainly, the respite is only fleeting as the circumstances usually persist.

These people are not trying to kill themselves, they are just trying to cope. If you know anyone in this position, there are many ways to help them. Firstly, let them know you are aware of their predicament, and that they can talk to you without judgement. Assure them that all discussions will remain private. Help them to locate a compassionate health professional for continuing assistance, and advise them about the reliable helplines where they'll be able to chat with a counsellor. Here's a list of less harmful things they or you could try when next feeling overwhelmed: Hold ice cubes in the hand as cold causes discomfort but is not harmful to health, wear a rubber band on the wrist and snap it when feeling the need, use a red pen to draw on the parts which would usually be cut, keep fit as a distraction; consume a chilli, scrawl on paper, try deep breathing and relaxation exercises. Attaching a photo of your protagonist to a dartboard, then firing darts at it can provide a sense of delight. Buying a punching bag will provide an outlet that anyone can beat the bejesus out of. Participants may even enjoy this form of physical activity. Encourage others to adopt a healthy lifestyle by avoiding or limiting their drug and alcohol usage, as these can exaggerate their negative feelings. If self-harm has already taken place, make sure the injuries are attended to as they will need to be cleaned and bandaged to avoid the risk of infection. Giving up self-harm and developing new habits for coping with extreme emotions can take time, but with copious help from professionals, kinsfolk, friends and colleagues, folks will ultimately progress from self-harm to self-help.

A number of sufferers will become so severely depressed that they will contemplate taking their own lives. They may have been thinking about this for a long time without sharing their feelings with anyone. In the past in Australia, suicide was considered a criminal offence, and whilst that is not the case now, it still is in many countries. There are many useful ways that we can help a person who is considering suicide. They will be at their lowest ebb, feeling utterly worthless and thinking there is no way out of their darkness. If you can, identify ways to calm them down when they are feeling overwhelmed. By helping them to control their emotions, they will be better equipped to cope with difficult situations. It is also important that you explain to them about the many trained professionals who are available to help them. Thus, you are building bridges, not barriers for them. It also helps to explain to them that although they are feeling utterly rotten right now, and have decided this really is a dog's life, these thoughts will pass and good times will return. Another sobering fact to relate to them is "your life is not simply all about you". Discuss the anguish that would be felt by their family, friends, colleagues and others, if they departed suddenly. This is a fact they may not have considered as they are not normally selfish by nature and should remind them they really are a worthwhile member of the group. By enrolling in a course to become an accredited mental health first-aider you will learn the practical skills to confidently help those in need. An internet search will provide the details about where to enrol.

The vast majority of those who attempt suicide are the targets of relentless bullying and harsh judgement. Bullying can cause long-term damage to self-esteem and increased risk of personality disorders, leading to social and emotional problems. These can reappear years after the bullying has stopped. Targets of this intimidating behaviour are mostly at a loss when deciding how to deal with the perpetrators. It has been shown that occasionally if you're being verbally taunted, you may be able to counteract this by fogging. Put simply, this means stay calm and self-possessed, and (appear to) agree with what they are saying. Then ask them to explain their point of view, which will probably shock them, optimistically making them back off. By reaching out and sharing your unhappy situation with somebody, be it family, friends or a professional, you are making a stand by asking for and (hopefully) receiving help, and not being frightened into submission. The reasons people bully others are varied and complex. They may be jealous of others, have family issues, or feel insecure, so they upset others to make themselves feel better. By making you feel inferior, they somehow consider they are superior. Nonetheless, this understanding in no way condones their contemptible behaviour. If you see any evidence of intimidatory behaviour, you must step in to stop it, or report it immediately. When left unchecked, hostile behavior could lead to criminality, relationship violence, child corruption and sexual aggravation. If you are guilty of oppressive behaviour, put this book down and seek help now. You need to realise that bullying is a behaviour you have learned so it can be readily unlearned. By understanding why you are doing it, you can resolve to reprogram your stress in other ways. You may need professional help, someone to listen to your concerns to help you get to the bottom of what is bothering you. They will help you to understand that when you put others down, you do not elevate yourself. The impact on the victim could be disastrous, as they may self-harm or attempt suicide, develop an eating disorder, or achieve lower grades, thus minimising their future prospects. It will become difficult for you to live with the consequences of what you've done. Each time you glance in a mirror a monster will be staring back at you. That's a hell of a burden for you to carry around. Best to get help pronto! Legally, you can be held accountable if you knowingly drive a person to suicide or if you do not step in to help when you know someone is in real danger of attempting to end their life.

In this modern age there are a multitude of bullying tactics including scamming. Scamming can occur via email, post or telephone. These unscrupulous individuals are not only bullies but can be considered thieves as well. Unfortunately, many individuals who have felt the brunt of these scams are left with little or no money and worse in debt. Many have borrowed huge sums to pay these individuals and some have been required to sell their home or declare bankruptcy. In such situations the prey is dealing with grief due in part to low self-worth, financial loss and left feeling overwhelmed and vulnerable. The mere thought of having been 'taken in' by these scoundrels leaves the victims feeling shameful and often they isolate themselves from their community and society in general.

Telcos should assist their many clients by putting a stop to this. It is heartening to learn that now they are putting more effort into finding and closing down these sites. You can bar the offending telephone numbers, but because they are usually fake numbers, they will ring again from a different number. By not answering calls from a private or unknown number, you greatly reduce your chances of being conned.

9

Coronavirus (COVID-19) SARS-CoV-2

Suddenly the world has become afflicted with the coronavirus, taking us all into uncharted territory. It has been described as a pandemic because it affects nations over a wide geographical area. The symptoms to be on the lookout for comprise flu-like symptoms incorporating sore throat, cough, nasal congestion, runny nose, high temperature, as well as fatigue, shortness of breath, loss of smell or hearing, chills, muscle aches and pains and headache. The incubation period, which is the time between catching it and showing symptoms, ranges from between one and fourteen days, the usual time being about five to six days. There is no known cure available, so treatment is aimed at making patients unperturbed while they recover. The measures suggested include adequate rest, drinking more fluids, small, frequent, nourishing meals and taking medication for the pain and fever. Those most likely at risk of dying from COVID-19 appear to be the elderly and those suffering from the following ailments – chronic kidney disease, heart disease, diabetes, immunocompromised illnesses and chronic lung disease. We're still learning about the many ways in which coronavirus impacts on our mental health. The advice is to stay alert, but not alarmed.

There is a wide-spread belief that coronavirus most likely originated in animals because it is similar to a virus that already exists in bats and pangolins, or scaly anteaters. How it transferred from animals to humans is not exactly known. What is known is that some of the early cases were connected to a live animal (wet) market in the Chinese city of Wuhan, in Hubei province. But we're not sure if this was the source, or if it's where it crossed over from animals to humans. Research has shown that bats host many viruses which can quickly spread in their colonies due to the close living environments, without seemingly affecting the bats themselves. One theory is that it spread from bats, via another animal, then on to the humans. Conversely, there have been a few reported cases where the infection has passed on to animals (cats, dogs and tigers) from humans. News has just surfaced claiming that COVID-19 may have appeared in Italy about three months earlier than the China outbreak. This knowledge is possible because of retroactive testing. This early outbreak may have been a different strain of the virus which has now become so widespread. Scientists are examining whole genome sequences of the virus to learn how it spreads and evolves, enabling them to comprehend how lockdowns affect the spreading of the virus. Researchers are further studying archived examples as they try to describe the timeline of the pandemic, making them well equipped for similar manifestations which may occur in the future.

As soon as COVID-19 was discovered, a plethora of conspiracy theories began emerging. This is largely because it is a very frightening time and people don't want to acknowledge that it exists. (Ostrich with head in sand again.) These theories range from it being a hoax, a bioweapon to give certain nations superiority, a ruse to distract us from a doomsday asteroid, and numerous other fanciful notions. In fact, there are over 100 websites dedicated to these extreme ideas. By now, most of us are fully aware of the reality of this coronavirus.

Some simple precautions we can all take to minimise our risk of contracting COVID-19 include regular hand-washing for at least twenty seconds with soap and warm water, or an alcohol based sanitiser, and avoiding touching our face with our hands. Shaking hands is now frowned upon. Many years ago, people shook hands to show they weren't carrying a weapon, but these days your hand could potentially be as dangerous as a weapon. It's being replaced with the elbow bump. Social distancing of at least 1.5 metres apart is recommended, so is regular cleaning and disinfecting of all surfaces in our homes. (As clean as a hound's tooth.) The wearing of face masks, especially in public, could also prevent us from catching and spreading this disease. If your area has to go into total lockdown, it is vital you follow the rules. They are not made to annoy you, rather they are designed to save your life.

Whilst you are following the above rules, you will undoubtedly become fed up and frustrated. It is estimated that more than half of Australians are stressed because of the coronavirus. The main concerns were not being able to see family and friends, and the uncertainty of keeping steady employment, which could result in losing their home and being unable to provide for the family or pay bills. The frequent handwashing may make them dry, requiring the application of moisturising cream on an on-going basis. Massaging them with olive oil will also rehydrate them. The process of desocialisation could make you feel lonely. Another fascinating global occurrence noticed at this time is 'Pandemic Dreaming' in which many people are experiencing sleep disturbances, dreaming about forbidden things and places, such as overseas travel, not disinfecting and meeting in large groups. There are even online sites where you can share your COVID dreams! Some of you will become infected with cabin fever, a highly nervous state resulting from being restrained in a cramped or confined space. Luckily it is the 21st century and most of us have internet access, so the communication lines are still open! Not the same as face to face, but safe and convenient. Essential shopping has been challenging, especially just prior to a lockdown taking effect. Some goods will be unavailable or in short supply due to disrupted transport arrangements. Panic buying more than you need is gratuitous and selfish.

You may become a casualty of the latest iteration of coronavirus without even contacting the disease. Consider the many unfortunate patients whose conditions worsened over the time it took to receive a diagnosis. Appointments held over the telephone or computer will never be as precise as face-to-face meetings. As the medicos made it known that COVID-19 was their top priority, many GP visits were delayed far too long. For months, elective surgery was put on hold. Really, how often is surgery actually elective? I say it's mostly essential.

As a result of being isolated over a period of time, there has been an increase in mental health problems, as dealing with this outbreak has made some of us want to break out! Here it is prudent to remember that being alone does not have to mean being lonely. Some folks have come up with ingenious ways to cope, including non-contact letterbox drops to loved ones containing notes, photos, drawings and messages of hope. Others revived the ancient art of letter writing by acquiring a penfriend from a distant area. Study, playing a musical instrument, undertaking craft projects or brushing up on a subject that had you perplexed at school are all popular options at this time. As distant tourism was not allowed, some families went camping in their own backyard, whilst others secretly hid Easter eggs in their neighbours' yards to surprise them. Also popular at this time is the opportunity to completely clean out your house, or shed, or car, etc. I recently viewed a delightful photo of two young boys, both about nine years old, perched in trees in their respective backyards, having a great chat whilst socially isolating! Several householders in our area have adorned their front windows with teddy bears and hand-drawn rainbows as a symbol of belief and confidence, looking forward to a better, healthier future.

What about the Easter bunny? Yes, animals can carry the COVID-19 virus, and some have caught it, so how come he or she or it, gets an exemption? Our state premier granted a G2G pass to Father Christmas and his pack of reindeers to deliver gifts on Christmas Eve (the Santa clause). Surely that was a risky decision, considering all the countries he travels through? Can recovering from the virus provide immunity? More studies need to be undertaken to find the answers to this, as, in a few rare cases, individuals have caught it more than once. This may have occurred because the virus strains were different. We're now hearing that around 45 percent of patients who supposedly recovered from the virus months ago still suffer from a degree of Covidity. These long COVID effects commonly include heart palpitations, cough, joint pain, 'brain fog', fatigue, depression, muscle pain, shortness of breath and chest pain. No matter how dire the circumstances, there is a definite need to let life flow and act maturely. If social occasions need to be curtailed by reducing numbers, then so be it. If the wedding, funeral, birthday party or other celebration turns out to be smaller than originally planned, suck it up and move on. Anzac services became virtual transmissions and home-schooling was practised, not by choice but through necessity as many schools closed for extended periods. The ambitious students managed fine but for many it was disastrous as they didn't have the necessary self-discipline, and some parents weren't capable of imitating teachers. When schools reopened, all extra-curricular activities were banned for a time, including excursions, sports days and social events. The students probably felt like they were given the cake without the icing! Instead of commuting to the office, many people worked from home, which proved to some extent difficult if they were home-schooling as well. Some enjoyed the experience, whilst others are not keen to repeat it! A lot of contact sports were cancelled, resulting in less exercise and fresh air for many of us.

The economy sure took a beating, with many businesses collapsing. Some were already teetering on the brink before COVID-19 appeared. Due to the cancellation of garage sales and clearing sales people were unable to sell off unwanted items, causing cash-flow problems, as well as running out of room to store the surplus items. The charity stores, whose foremost volunteers are elderly and therefore at high risk of contracting the virus, were all closed as well, meaning no cheap shopping either. Of course, like in all disasters, there were some traders who flourished in the new conditions. It was hard to ignore the unending news of the pandemic, resulting in an increased state of anxiety for many of us.

The future is looking a lot brighter now. Australia's first shipments of COVID-19 vaccinations have arrived and immunisation has now started. Over 60 percent of Australians have indicated they will take part in the program which involves receiving two injections several weeks apart. However, trials are underway on a vaccination which is said to only require one dose.

10

Facing the Future with Optimism

Moving forward is a natural progression. "I want to live before I die." This is a significant statement to acknowledge. Use it as your daily mantra to keep you motivated. What do you enjoy doing? Be realistic here. Decide what really matters. Pick activities that are attainable, despite them requiring a massive effort. Commitment, motivation and perseverance will keep you going. With the right attitude, your days will be better. Expect the best but prepare for the worst. There will still be down days but you will have the expertise to manage them, and there will be less of them. You may not be perfect, but you'll be okay. (Every dog has his day.) As you overcome 'the blues' you will gain a new-found confidence. You will need to take a decisive role in order to determine actions. An important step towards this is making time for yourself. Sometimes others will expect too much of you so you must learn to say no and stick to your decision. This can be done politely by saying, "Thanks for asking me, but I'm unavailable." You don't need to give any further explanation.

If you have been wronged big time, you needn't become a martyr, and don't ever 'play the victim'. There are always choices. An old saying goes like this: Don't get mad, get even. Though, if you can do both, why not? (Another saying: Candy is sweet. Revenge is sweeter.) At first, you'll most likely become angry and want to yell out a few expletives. This is actually a therapeutic release for you, but choose where you do it! If you do this often, you could consider having a swear-jar on the cupboard, putting in some money each time you utter a naughty word. When it has sufficient funds you could donate it to a charity, thus enhancing your mood by being generous. Now for getting even. If your parents have wronged you, gently remind them that you'll probably get a say in choosing their aged-care facility. If it's your spouse, destroy the wedding photos along with that awful gift from their relatives. Your offspring did it? Spend their inheritance. Perhaps it was the grandkids? Then give them another chance, (and another, then another) as they are only young and still learning. If it was a shop assistant that treated you with utter disdain, dragging you down, making you feel lower than a snake's belly, take your grievances to management. They will most likely address the issue and come up with an apology and suitable outcome as it is in their best interests to do so. If not, you take your business (and your dollars) elsewhere. Always be mindful that when anyone yells and screams at you it may have more to do with them than you. We'll never really know what sort of a life they're having, so you could acknowledge that they are unhappy and ask if there's anything you can do to help. Understanding comes from being non-judgemental as we're only seeing their situation from our perspective. No matter what you've heard, remember there are at least two sides to the story. No-one expects you to fix all problems, and at times taking a deep breath and walking away is what is needed. Taking a suitably long saunter will remove you from the situation, helping to put things into perspective, and the fresh air outdoors will enhance your state of mind. We must acknowledge that some individuals wish to figure things out alone. Their decision should be accepted and we need to back off graciously.

A well-developed sense of humour is a great coping mechanism which will considerably optimise your happiness. It makes dark situations appear lighter and adds fun and nonsense into our lives. It provides a great counter-balance to the (sometimes) harsh realities of life. Think of it as your safety valve, to save you from blowing a gasket! Never underestimate the importance of make-believe in your life. It is much too important to be utilised only by children! May we never grow too old for flights of fancy and figments of our imagination. Look upon this as dreaming whilst awake! An amazing scientific fact states that the brain cannot tell the difference between fantasy and reality. An added bonus is that fantasy doesn't need to be logical! If you let a menagerie of impish gremlins into your home you'll never again be blamed for putting the car keys in the fridge, or discovering the remote control in the bath! Of course their cousins the goblins, will take up residence in your garden and will occasionally rearrange the gnomes, maybe decapitate a few! No matter how old you are, it is possible to remain young at heart. You really should aim to be funny/silly at least part of each day, as it tends to keep us sane - or someplace reasonably close to it.

What would make your life truly happy? "I want to become rich and famous," is a common reply. Really? But, what do they actually mean? Anyone can be rich without having great vaults of money. They may have found their true purpose in life and revel in the knowledge that they are surrounded by honest, loving people. If they mean monetary rich, then of course most of us wouldn't complain if we were a bit more financially comfortable, but anything more would be greedy. Beware, the trappings of wealth can be as debilitating as the trappings of poverty. As for the famous bit, no thank you. Visualise no anonymity. When you venture out, reporters are lurking about, ready to record your moves, to repeat your words. Incidentally, a large proportion of so-called famous mortals suffer from mental illnesses, same as us common folk. Whatever their status and wealth, they are flesh and blood just like the rest of us, with the same problems, uncertainties and challenges. Some may appear to be more important/successful/famous than you, but you're only witnessing a superficial part of their existence. There is no need to worship others. Remember that basically we're quite alike. It makes no sense at all to lionise someone for doing well in their chosen occupation. They are (usually) paid well for their efforts. This certainly applies to professional sports players, actors and musicians. In fact, the more you put your faith (and hopes/wishes/dreams) in others, the less effort you will make for yourself. Have you ever prayed earnestly for something, then it never eventuated? Praying appears to be another form of outsourcing. It would have been a more favourable outcome had you put more effort into doing it yourself. Beware the bulldust. Be yourself. It's the only constant you have, and no-one knows you better!

Let's examine that popular furphy - the bucket list. If you stick to an outdated list you've had for years, you'll only drag yourself down. Some of the list of contents were applicable many moons ago, being childhood dreams, but hopefully you've grown a lot since then and now have totally different ideas, which is understandable and healthy. How long have some items been on the list? If you haven't done them yet there's probably a reasonable explanation why not. Best plan here is to shred the list (papier-mâché dove is optional) and act impulsively.

When you surround yourself with positive people, you are increasing your quality of life continually. By assessing the folks you come into usual contact with, you'll soon learn which ones to discard. Look upon this as stock-taking as no-one has the right to hijack your happiness. Sadly, there will be occasions when you encounter toxic, permanently pessimistic individuals. On these occasions, it's best for you to build a mental barrier between you and them. Happy, gregarious companions will encourage you to let your light shine. With their backing, your pilot light will rapidly become a floodlight. You will encounter numerous pot-holes on the road to self-discovery. There will be many red lights, and you'll have to give way regularly, perhaps need to take a detour or two, but as your journey progresses the road ahead will become smoother, the lights will turn green and you'll have a hell of a ride! This is the only life we can be certain of. There is no guarantee of another. So give it your best shot before the big full stop. You and I are quite alike.

Acknowledgement

I truly appreciate the learned academics and the delightful yoga ladies who have freely shared their vast knowledge with me, with the understanding that we are altogether contributing to the betterment of our fellow human beings.

www.ingramcontent.com/pod-product-compliance
Lightning Source LLC
Chambersburg PA
CBHW071410290426
44108CB00014B/1763